One Hundred Valid Reasons to Be an Atheist

DONOVAN G. NEWKIRK

One Hundred Valid Reasons to Be an Atheist

ISBN: 979-8-218-38866-9

This book is dedicated to my father, Donald H. Newkirk, Jr.
I am grateful for his patience and his love. He taught me how to be a man, how to be a father, and, most importantly, how to be a follower of Christ.

This book is also dedicated to Senior Pastor Jonathan Falwell.
Serving as a lighting technician on the technical production team at Thomas Road Baptist Church has been, and will forever be, one of the greatest and most humbling experiences of my life.

Table of Contents

Reason

1

Reason

2

Reason

3

Reason

4

Reason

5

Reason

6

Reason

7

Reason

8

Reason

9

Reason

10

Reason

11

Reason

12

Reason

13

Reason

14

Reason

15

Reason

16

Reason

17

Reason

18

Reason

19

Reason

20

Reason

21

Reason

22

Reason

23

Reason

24

Reason

25

Reason

26

Reason

27

Reason

28

Reason

29

Reason

30

Reason

31

Reason

32

Reason

33

Reason

34

Reason

35

Reason

36

Reason

37

Reason

38

Reason

39

Reason

40

Reason

41

Reason

42

Reason

43

Reason

44

Reason

45

Reason

46

Reason

47

Reason

48

Reason

49

Reason

50

Reason

51

Reason

52

Reason

53

Reason

54

Reason

55

Reason

56

Reason

57

Reason

58

Reason

59

Reason

60

Reason

61

Reason

62

Reason

63

Reason

64

Reason

65

Reason

66

Reason

67

Reason

68

Reason

69

Reason

70

Reason

71

Reason

72

Reason

73

Reason

74

Reason

75

Reason

76

Reason

77

Reason

78

Reason

79

Reason

80

Reason

81

Reason

82

Reason

83

Reason

84

Reason

85

Reason

86

Reason

87

Reason

88

Reason

89

Reason

90

Reason

91

Reason

92

Reason

93

Reason

94

Reason

95

Reason

96

Reason

97

Reason

98

Reason

99

Reason

100

About the Author:

DONOVAN G. NEWKIRK is a third-year law student at Liberty University School of Law. He has an interest in taxation law, intellectual property law, and securities regulation law. He is the president of Liberty University School of Law's Intellectual Property Clinic, and he is currently serving as a research assistant for Professor of Law Jeffrey C. Tuomala. After graduating from law school in the Spring of 2024, Donovan will be attending Georgetown Law Center's Taxation LL.M. Program.

Donovan was born in Buffalo, New York (but he has since emphatically renounced his New York residency and now considers himself a full-fledged Virginian). He graduated with a bachelor's degree in political science from the University at Buffalo in May of 2020. Shortly thereafter, he and his wife moved to Arlington, Virginia, where he began working in conservative media. He was a 2020 *College Fix* fellow and interned with *RealClearPolitics'* education division, RealClearEducation, where he reported on instances of leftist bias on college campuses throughout the United States. After that, he interned at the Media Research Center, where he wrote for *NewBusters* and reported on the pervasiveness of left-wing bias in the media, particularly on cable news channels like CNN, ABC, and MSNBC.

He began his law school career at Mississippi College School of Law, but transferred after his first year because he was treated poorly by his professors and colleagues for being both a Christian and a conservative.

Website: DonovanNewkirk.com

Other Books:
The War on Terror: How Lawyers Have Kept America Safe

In Preparation:
Intellectual Property Law & Taxation: How the Government Benefits from Creativity

A Household Divided: The Importance of the Paterfamilias

www.ingramcontent.com/pod-product-compliance
Lightning Source LLC
Chambersburg PA
CBHW030416100426
42812CB00028B/2981/J